FOR THE LOVE OF
CATS

FOR THE LOVE OF CATS

First published in 2015 as *Cats: A Miscellany*
This revised and updated edition copyright © Summersdale Publishers
Ltd, 2017

With research by Anna Maria Espsäter

Illustrations © Shutterstock

Summersdale Publishers Ltd
46 West Street
Chichester
West Sussex
PO19 1RP
UK

www.summersdale.com

Printed and bound in the Czech Republic

ISBN: 978-1-78685-031-7

Substantial discounts on bulk quantities of Summersdale books are available
to corporations, professional associations and other organisations. For
details contact general enquiries: telephone: +44 (0) 1243 771107, fax:
+44 (0) 1243 786300 or email: enquiries@summersdale.com.

FOR THE LOVE OF
CATS

KATE MAY

summersdale

CONTENTS

INTRODUCTION

There are many reasons why we find cats so fascinating. Their individual personalities, their curiosity and sheer grace, plentiful purrs and ample affection (when bestowed) joyously enrich our lives.

That said, we know comparatively little about them. Their very independence and aloofness, which can sometimes come across as downright disdain, are interesting and appealing character traits. On the whole, our feline companions are discerning; they don't just shower every Tom, Dick and Harry with their affections. Instead they take their time, check you out, sniff you, consider you and eventually decide whether they deem you worthy.

The chapters in this book endeavour to capture some of the many joys that cats can bring and explain some of those quirky cat habits. Many cats, from the well known, well loved and heroic to the unknown, unsung and plain, wander through these pages. We look at the history of how our domestic moggies came to grace our homes and lives with their presence, the etymology of the word 'cat' and many of the popular cat phrases in use today and in the past.

The Egyptians might have started the trend of cat worship, but today we are arguably in the midst of a new era of looking up to our feline friends, with an estimated half a billion cats sharing our lives around the globe. Our love of cats extends into popular culture, literature, music and television, where they are the focus of our attention, and on the internet, postings of funny cat photos, GIFs and memes abound – we have chapters to cover their popularity across all media, where some famous felines are singled out. Going back in time, there's a brief look at historically famous cats and famed ailurophiles, as well as mythological felines. Cats feature extensively in folkloric beliefs and superstition, with some surprisingly similar folk tales concerning cats in different parts of the world.

Above all, the book aims to be a celebration of all things cat, the four-pawed friend that we know and love. Sprinkled throughout the book are quirky cat facts and figures along with cat feats, cat celebrities and scientific information if you're curious to find out more about your favourite moggy. Finally, the book includes a list of further reading and useful websites for follow-up. Happy reading!

THE HISTORY OF DOMESTICATION

The phrase 'domestic cat'
is an oxymoron.

GEORGE F. WILL

FROM WILDCATS TO PETS

Cats have a long history: there is fossil evidence of African wildcats going back 38 million years. The domestic cat was first classified by the Swedish botanist Carl Linnaeus (later ennobled and known as Carl von Linné) in 1758 as *Felis catus*. Although cats have been domesticated and shared their lives with humans for centuries (it's only in the past 60 to 70 years that they have moved from a mostly outdoor life to a more indoor-based lifestyle with fewer hunting and wild traits), the domestication process has been slow. Our domestic moggy, science tells us, is only a few gene mutations away from their wilder ancestors.

TIGER, TIGER

Global or International Tiger Day has been celebrated worldwide on 29 July since 2010 to raise public awareness of tiger conservation issues. India is the country with the highest number of wild tigers, estimated at just over 1,700.

THE FIRST CATS – OUR CATS' ANCESTORS

Felidae is the common biological name for the cat family, divided into two subfamilies: the Pantherinae, which includes many of the wilder species, and the Felinae, which also includes wild species such as lynx, cougar, cheetah and ocelot, as well as our domestic cat. It's believed that all felids shared a common ancestor as little as ten to fifteen million years ago. Over the past ten million years, big cats and domestic cats have continued to diverge, but looking at the DNA make-up, there are a surprising amount of similarities among all the members of the felid family. From three million years ago, wildcat species were found around the globe, with the exception of the least hospitable areas, such as Antarctica and the Arctic. There are 36 or 37 (though some sources report 41) species of felids today.

BIG CATS

There are five members of the Pantherinae subfamily referred to as 'big cats' – lion, tiger, jaguar, leopard and snow leopard. These impressive kitties are the only ones that have the ability to roar. The lion is one of the few social felids, living in groups known as prides, but on the whole cats big or small tend to be solitary. Remarkable though it seems, the world's big cats, whose lives couldn't be more different from your average domestic moggy's, share over 95 per cent of the same DNA, according to a 2013 study by an international team of scientists. Tigers are the largest members of the cat family, lions the tallest.

CATS IN RELIGION

The Torah, the Jewish religious text, mostly has references to big cats – lions, tigers and leopards – while the Talmud, the book of Jewish law, references the humbler house cat. If God had not given Jewish people the Torah, it states, they would have learned modesty from the cat and this is one of several 'cat mentions' in the text. On the whole, cats in Jewish communities flourished in the Middle Ages, a time when Jews were being demonised and killed by Christians.

The holy book of Islam, the Koran or Qur'an, has by far the most mentions of cats, and both the prophet Muhammad and one of his companions Abu Hurayrah (sometimes spelled Hurairah), which means 'father of kittens', appear to have been avid cat lovers. Muhammad very much cared for his favourite cat Muezza, who takes centre stage in several stories. Islam teaches that people should look after cats well and mistreating a cat is considered a serious sin.

God made the cat in order that man might have the pleasure of caressing the lion.

FERNAND MÉRY

TOP FIVE LARGEST CAT SPECIES IN THE WORLD

1. Largest in the cat kingdom is the Siberian tiger. On average, this tiger reaches about two metres (80 inches) in length and can weigh as much as 425 kilograms (just under 1,000 pounds). These gorgeous creatures that roam the snowy plains of Russia are under serious threat, with only some 400 left in the world today, although exact figures are hazy.

2. The lion may not be the largest big cat, but it's still the tallest, averaging 120 centimetres (4 feet) for a male and 110 centimetres (3 feet 6 inches) for a female, and weighing in at 127 kilograms (280 pounds) for females, and 190 kilograms (420 pounds) for males. There are now eight recognised subspecies of lion, and they can be found across Africa.

3. The jaguar is the only panther species found in the Americas, and although only the third largest of the cat species in the world,

it's the largest in the western hemisphere. Its territory stretches from southwestern USA right down to Argentina, with the rainforest as its preferred habitat. The jaguar is one of the few cat species that enjoys swimming.

4. The puma, also known as cougar or mountain lion, is the one big cat that most resembles the smaller feline species in looks. Fond of mountains in a territory that ranges from southern Canada to the tip of South America, the puma has a thick coat to keep it warm in the often freezing, high altitude temperatures. The puma is one of the most adaptable predators – although preferring the mountains, its habitats can include deserts, grasslands, forests and even jungles.

5. The smallest of the five big cats is the leopard, part of the panther genus. It's found, in declining numbers, across large parts of Africa and Asia and is similar in appearance to other large, spotted cats, including the cheetah and the jaguar. Somewhat confusingly, both black leopards and black jaguars are known as black panthers.

WILDCATS

Some nine million years ago, the big cats branched off the evolutionary line, and fossilised evidence tells us that small wildcat species have been in existence since then. Our human-friendly felines are direct descendants of, and very similar to, small wildcats that populated large parts of the planet three million years ago. The classification *Felis silvestris catus* now refers to both domestic cats and wildcats, such as the Scottish wildcat. There are seven species of wildcat today, depending on the classifying body (various scientific and academic bodies classify them differently), including European and African wildcat, the jungle cat, Chinese mountain cat and Arabian sand cat. Over millennia and to this day, there has been much interbreeding between domestic and wildcats – even experts find it hard to tell them apart just by looking. Wildcats, on the whole, are extremely shy around humans, and the main difference between wild and domestic is that of temperament, the wilder relatives remaining far more aggressive than your average lap cat at home.

Her function is to sit
and be admired.

GEORGINA STRICKLAND GATES

TOP FIVE SMALLEST NON-DOMESTIC CAT SPECIES IN THE WORLD

There are 19 different wild species of cats in the world that qualify as 'small cat' species.

1. The rusty-spotted cat, found in India and Sri Lanka, is the smallest cat species in the world, at just 35–48 centimetres (14–19 inches) in length with a weight between 0.9–1.6 kilograms (2.0–3.5 pounds). There are currently less than 10,000 left in the world.

2. The black-footed (also called small-spotted) cat is the smallest African cat species, reaching a maximum length of 43.3 centimetres (17 inches), while weighing up to 2.45 kilograms (5.4 pounds) for males, the female being slightly smaller. Found in the sub-Saharan region, it is on the list of vulnerable species.

3. Across the Atlantic, the kodkod, also known as güiña, is the smallest species in the Americas. Brownish-yellow in

colour, with darker spots, it's only found in southern and central Chile and the borders of Argentina. There are less than 10,000 alive today.

4. Also in the Americas, the oncilla, or tiger cat, is native to the tropical rainforests of Central and South America. Longer and lighter than a domestic cat, the oncilla is a close relation to the ocelot and margay. It's almost completely nocturnal and an excellent climber.

5. The flat-headed cat, from South East Asia, lives up to its name. It's distinguished by the depression of its skull, making its head look flatter than that of other species. Reddish-brown fur and large canine teeth are also distinguishing characteristics. There are thought to be only 2,500 flat-headed cats left in the world today.

EARLY DOMESTICATION

Cats began their journey towards domestication when humans began settling and farming some 10,000 years ago. The cats provided excellent mice and vermin control for the farmers, protecting their grain storages, and in turn they received a plentiful and regular supply of food. It's believed that gene mutations occurred over a long period of acclimatisation that made the cat tamer and less aggressive towards humans. There is evidence of domesticated cats in farming communities from Egypt to the Middle East and China over different eras BCE.

In Egypt, cats were particularly well looked after, worshipped and adored, something cat lovers argue that the cat has never forgotten. While there is evidence of felines in Egypt going as far back as 3000 BCE, the cat cult focusing on the goddess Bast, also known as Bastet or Pasht, began gaining importance around 940 BCE and remained strong until banned by decree some 400 years later. They were not as popular everywhere in ancient times – cats are, for example, almost entirely absent from the Bible, where they only get a single mention in Baruch 6:21 in the Eastern Orthodox and Catholic bibles.

CATS TAKE ON EUROPE

Despite a ban on the sale and export of cats from Egypt, the temptation was too great for Egyptian traders, even though they risked the death penalty if caught. They took cats to the Greeks and Romans around 1000 BCE where, as in Egypt, they were used for pest control in their new homes. Although they were not as revered as in their homeland, they were nonetheless well loved and cherished, particularly in Rome. Unlike many other now domestic animals, cats refused to be tamed and rather did things in their own fashion and on their own terms, learning to tolerate humans along the way. There was never a question of cats nearing extinction and having to throw in their lot with humans in order to survive, which was the case for certain species. Instead, they developed a mutually beneficial relationship with humans and from there they started to spread across Europe.

THE CYPRUS CAT

A now famous, though nameless, cat was found buried next to a human in a Neolithic grave in Cyprus in 2004, turning the whole domestication theory on its head, given that it was some 6,000 years older than the domestic cats found buried in Egypt. The cat in question, estimated to be about eight months old, was much larger than today's domestic cat and resembled an African wildcat. Scientists believe it to be predomesticated, somewhere between wild and tame. It was buried together with a person of unknown gender.

THE VIKINGS

Generally, evidence suggests that cats didn't migrate over large distances of their own accord, but instead were taken to places by humans, travelling overland or by boat. By 100 CE domestic cats had reached the British Isles, in all likelihood with the Romans. When the Vikings arrived some 700 years later, they were thought to have brought cats from their native lands, as well as having taken cats from the British Isles back with them and using both kinds of cat as mousers on their ships to protect their food supplies. These cats in turn met other cats, so although the Vikings aren't known for their cat fancying tendencies, they might accidentally have helped create a new breed, the Norwegian Forest cat. Other theories go even further and believe the Vikings took cats across the Atlantic to modern-day USA and Canada, but there's little actual evidence of any of them surviving on the other side of the pond.

THE NEW WORLD

The Spanish conquistadors, in their search for new and fertile lands to plunder rather like the earlier Vikings, were responsible for bringing the first domestic cats to the Americas (although there were already wildcat species in existence here beforehand). Further north, in the USA and Canada, many of today's native population of cats are of northern European ancestry, brought over by British, French and Scandinavian colonists. Interestingly, polydactyl cats – cats that are born with more than the usual number of toes on one or more paws – are more abundant along the east coast of North America because they were very popular as ship's cats and many were brought to North America from Britain. Polydactyl cats are also more plentiful in southwest England and across Wales. Australia and Antarctica are the only continents with no indigenous domestic feline species.

GEOFFROY'S CAT

Geoffroy's cat, named after French naturalist Geoffroy Saint-Hilaire, is a small wildcat native to southern and central South America. About the same size as a domestic cat, Geoffroy's cat looks like a small leopard, as it has the same distinctive black spots. Unusually, this wildcat is able to stand on its hind legs to survey its surroundings, using its tail for added support and balance. It's the second most common cat species in South America after the ocelot.

TOP TEN COUNTRIES WITH THE HIGHEST ESTIMATED DOMESTIC CAT POPULATION

Note: the figures have been rounded up

1. USA – 76.5 million
2. China – 53 million
3. Russia – 13 million
4. Brazil – 12.5 million
5. France – 10 million
6. Italy – 9.5 million
7. UK – 8 million
8= Ukraine – 7.5 million
8= Japan – 7.5 million
10. Germany – 7 million

THE SCOTTISH WILDCAT

Fossilised remains of wildcats in the British Isles date back over two million years. The Scottish wildcat, Britain's only remaining large, wild predator, is teetering on the brink of extinction, with only some 100 wildcats left today in the Scottish Highlands. These thick-coated tabby lookalikes are not feral cats but a different cat species altogether, predating the arrival of domestic cats to the British Isles. The coat is striped, black and brown, with a ruffled appearance due to its thickness, and with their big, fluffy tails, wildcats look deceptively cute. Don't be deceived – the wildcat is a fierce hunter with razor-sharp teeth and claws, hunting mostly at dawn and dusk. They shy away from humans at all costs and although a wildcat can purr, you'll never hear it meow. While the numbers of wildcat remain small, the number of feral cats roaming the Highlands is estimated at roughly 100,000 and this is by far the greatest threat to the wildcat species, as cross-mating is common.

FERAL OR STRAY?

Stray cats are pet cats that have been lost or abandoned. Feral cats are born in the wild. A feral cat has essentially never been socialised, or accustomed to humans, and is living in a wild state. Feral cats often live in colonies, sometimes in large numbers, and as such are able to live well in to ripe old age, while lone feral cats don't fare quite as well. They differ from wildcats in that they have domestic ancestry; for example, the offspring of a stray could be considered feral. Stray cats, on the other hand, have been used to the company and care of humans and are usually first generation lost or abandoned domestic cats. They tend to attempt to stay near homes and other populated areas, although they may be fearful of people and can adopt feral behaviours over a period of time. Both feral and stray cats have the capacity to become used to humans again, although in the case of feral cats this is more likely to happen successfully if the cat is very young.

FASCINATING FELINE FACTS

Thirty per cent of US households have one or more cats, and around 35 per cent have been acquired as strays.

Twenty-six per cent of UK homes have one or more cats. Of those, 58 per cent have one cat, 29 per cent have two, seven per cent have three and six per cent have four or more cats.

Gallup research has found men and women are equally likely to have a cat.

Cats outnumber dogs by two to one as Ireland's most popular pet, 2014 figures suggest.

The feline with the most fearsome teeth is the clouded leopard. Its teeth can measure 4.5 centimetres (1.8 inches).

Cats have five toes on their front paws, but only four on their back paws.

Thirty-two muscles control the outer ear of a cat, while a human ear only has six.

There are 230 bones in a cat's body, compared to the 206 found in your average human.

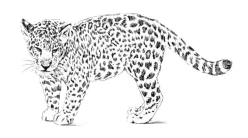

TIMELINE

38 million years ago – first fossil evidence of African wildcats

12–9 million years ago – cat species diverge

3 million years ago – wildcats populate the globe

10,000 years ago – cats begin to associate with humans in farming communities

9,500 years ago – cat buried next to a human in a grave in Cyprus

3,000 years ago – Egyptian cat cult at Bubastis and cats smuggled into Greece and Italy

1,900 years ago – domestic cats arrive in the British Isles

500 years ago – domestic cats arrive in the Americas (although some suggest the Vikings had brought cats earlier)

CAT LANGUAGE

There is, incidentally, no way of talking about cats that enables one to come off as a sane person.

DAN GREENBERG

WORDS FROM CATS

The word for 'cat' is remarkably similar in many different languages throughout the world, whether Latin-based or otherwise. Cats have also done their best to infiltrate our language and feature heavily in everyday phrases and popular expressions. This chapter looks at the history of the word itself and some of the many idioms associated with cats in the English language.

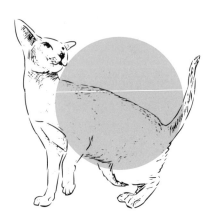

WHAT'S IN A NAME?

The modern English word 'cat' can be traced back to the late Latin word *Cattus*, which in turn has its roots in the late Egyptian word *čaute* and North African *quattah*. Many of today's European languages, including those as far apart geographically as Portuguese and Lithuanian, use words similar to the Latin word *Cattus*. There are very few exceptions to these etymologically similar words worldwide, from the Basque *catua* to Afrikaans *kat*. Notable exceptions are some of the Asian and Eastern European languages such as Vietnamese *(meo)* and Slovak *(mačka)*. The word 'kitten' stems from the old French word *chitoun*, the diminutive of the French word for cat, *chat*. In the past, *catling* was used in early modern English to mean the same thing.

'CAT' IN DIFFERENT LANGUAGES

Arabic – *qitta*

Basque – *katu*

Catalan – *gat*

Chinese – *mao*

Esperanto – *kato*

Finnish – *kissa*

French – *chat*

German – *katze*

Greek – *gata/gato*

Hebrew – *chatul*

Hindi – *billi*

Icelandic – kisa/*köttur*

Inuktitut – *pussi*

Italian – *gatto*

Japanese – *neko*

Norwegian – *katt*

Portuguese – *gato*

Russian – *koht/ kohsh-kuh*

Spanish – *gato*

Swahili – *paka*

Swedish – *katt*

Thai – *maa-oh*

Turkish – *kedi*

Welsh – *cath*

Zulu – *ikati*

MOGGIES AND MOUSERS

The domestic cat has picked up a fair few nicknames over the centuries. One of the most commonly used in the United Kingdom is 'moggy' or 'mog', usually referring to your average, non-pedigree cat, whether house cat or stray. The origins of the word are somewhat hazy. Although it is often mistakenly believed to be an abbreviation of mongrel, this is actually not the case. In fact, moggy appears to have been an affectionate term for a cow in rural Britain in the nineteenth century. In the cities, it came to refer to older, unkempt women, possibly a corruption of the female name Margaret and it was only in 1911 that the word moggy was first recorded as referring to a cat.

Another popular cat term in the UK is 'mouser', bringing to mind the phrase 'you are what you eat'. Cats that have honed their mouse-catching skills often attract this nickname and 'mouser' is one of the oldest recorded words used for a cat, going back to the 1400s.

GRIMALKIN

Grimalkin, or malkin, has Shakespeare to thank for its inception into cat lore and this word is often used to describe an older female cat. 'Gri' is a corruption of grey, while 'malkin' is the diminutive form of the name Malde, an earlier form of Maude or Matilda. Shakespeare included the grey cat Graymalkin, as the First Witch's familiar in his 1605 play *Macbeth* and the name has stood the test of time, staying continually in usage over the centuries, interchangeably referring to an older female cat or an older woman. Both were associated with magic and witchcraft and the name often appears in folklore and legends.

THE PUSS AND THE TOM

The words puss, pussy and pussycat are common in several European languages and appear in English from the early sixteenth century onwards. One theory explains that it derives from the Egyptian word 'Pasht', an alternative name of the cat goddess Bast or Bastet. Similar to the case of grimalkin, by the seventeenth century puss or pussy was also used to refer to a woman, but in this case a younger girl or maiden. Surprisingly, pussy was also a synonym for rabbits and hares in the past.

If grimalkin is always a female cat, the tom or tomcat is always a male. The name Tom for a male kitten dates back centuries, but actually referring to male cats as 'tomcats' was probably popularised much later, after the publication of 1760 children's book *The Life and Adventures of a Cat*, commonly attributed to William Guthrie, featuring Tom the Cat.

KNOW YOUR CAT TERMINOLOGY

- A group of cats is referred to as a clowder or a glaring of cats.

- Male cats, particularly unneutered, are known as toms or tomcats, while females are sometimes called mollies, or queens, if unneutered.

- Long before the current reading device entered present-day vocabulary, a group of kittens was known as a 'kindle', an expression that's now all but obsolete.

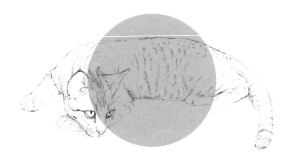

THE STRIPY TABBY

It is believed that the word 'tabby' hails from a neighbourhood in Baghdad, Iraq, called Attabiyah, famous for producing wavy-patterned silk. The stripy coats of the tabby cat resembled the silk patterns and hence gave the tabby its name.

SECRET SIGNIFICANCE

The short and sweet word 'cat' manages to squeeze in multiple definitions, ranging from the entirely logical to the downright obscure. Mixing up cats and women appears to be a long-standing habit and back in the thirteenth century you might use cat as an offensive term for a malicious woman, something that's lingered on to this day, for example in the usage of 'catty behaviour'.

Moving ahead a few hundred years to the early fifteenth century and cat had come to also mean a prostitute. There are nautical, computer, jazz and even drug trade 'cat terms' that have all come about in more recent times. Meanwhile, for the cat's nicknames you will find a whole plethora of other hidden meanings. A kitty has come to mean a 'pool of money' for sharing expenses; a sixteenth-century malkin was also a scarecrow; tomcatting means being on the prowl for sex, while puss or pussy has acquired numerous lewder meanings over the centuries. Cat is even used to refer to bad weather ('the weather was cat', mostly used in Ireland).

Lettin' the cat out of the bag is a whole lot easier 'n puttin' it back in.

WILL ROGERS

CURIOSITY KILLED THE CAT

From catcall and catwalk to cat burglar and copycat, our feline friends have well and truly penetrated the English language. Cats have gone through several bad patches with humans and were vilified throughout the Middle Ages, so it's perhaps no surprise that many cat expressions are less than flattering – fat cat, alley cat and scaredy-cat to name but a few. Characteristics traditionally ascribed to a cat, such as stealth, sneakiness, curiosity and a penchant for creature comforts, can often be found lurking behind some of the well-known expressions. The proverb 'curiosity killed the cat' used to warn of the dangers of unnecessary investigations, hails from Ben Jonson's late sixteenth-century play *Every Man in His Humour* in which Shakespeare was cast. 'The cat that got the cream', 'fighting like cats and dogs' and 'catnapping' are just some of the many other cat-sprinkled sayings in the English language.

CAT GOT YOUR TONGUE?

The phrase 'cat got your tongue?' is a rather roundabout way of asking someone why he or she is silent. Not quite as much in use these days, it's still one of many colloquial cat expressions that linger in English. It may be referring to the ancient, rather gruesome, punishment of cutting off a criminal's tongue and feeding it to the king's pets.

Another interesting turn of phrase still in use today is the mid-seventeenth-century 'Not enough room to swing a cat' to describe an enclosed, confined or awkwardly small space. There is some debate about the origins of this expression, but the oldest recorded sources hail from Elizabethan times, when cats were literally strung up in bags and used for archery practice – our poor feline friends have been much abused at the hands of humans.

The cat is the mirror of
his human's mind.

WINIFRED CARRIÈRE

QUIRKY CAT PHRASES AND EXPRESSIONS

Caterwauling – making shrill, howling noises

As much chance as a wax cat in hell or a cat-in-hell chance – in other words, no chance whatsoever

A cat in gloves catches no mice – being polite and timid won't necessarily allow you to accomplish your goals

Glamour puss – a glamorous-looking woman

Catnap – a short sleep

Let sleeping cats lie – leave things as they are

Cat's whiskers, cat's meow or cat's pyjamas – something that is considered outstanding

Having kittens – losing one's temper, going ballistic

Sourpuss – someone who is cranky or unfriendly

Like herding cats – a futile effort

Put the cat amongst the pigeons – to cause a flap, often by revealing a hidden fact or secret

Live a cat and dog life – to always be arguing

Weak as a kitten – weak, fragile and useless

CAT BEHAVIOUR AND COMMUNICATION

🐾🐾🐾🐾🐾🐾🐾🐾🐾🐾

There are few things in life
more heart-warming than
being welcomed by a cat.

TAY HOHOFF

🐾🐾🐾🐾🐾🐾🐾🐾🐾🐾

CATTY CONVERSATION

Why do cats behave the way they do and how do cats communicate? These fascinating areas are currently the subjects of a great deal of scientific study. Cats use sight, sound, smell and touch for communication, making them far more versatile than your average human. This chapter outlines some of the cat's key behaviours, including those most and least loved by their human companions.

PURR-FECT MEOWS

Ask anyone to name a typical cat sound and the purr is often the first that springs to mind, despite the louder and more frequent meow. A cat's purr is one of the most soothing sounds imaginable, even though a cat doesn't purr solely when happy and content, but also when distressed or in pain (see next page, What's in a Purr?). You rarely hear of a 'purring lion', but the wilder of the cat species can also produce a sound similar to purring, besides its more famous roaring abilities. Cats produce a whole range of different sounds (as many as 15 sounds and 60 different notes) accompanied by body language to communicate. Although kittens mew to their mothers, meowing is not used between adults. Instead adult cats tend to direct their meows in various intonations towards humans to express a variety of emotions. Who hasn't succumbed to a plaintive, complaining, attention-seeking, demanding or downright cute meow from his or her favourite feline?

WHAT'S IN A PURR?

Exactly how cats produce that distinctive feline sound known as purring remains a scientific mystery, and neither has the purpose of the purr been definitely determined. As kittens, the combination of purring and paddling their mother's belly with their tiny front paws is thought to induce the milk let-down reflex and enable them to suckle. Grown-up cats may purr when relaxed and contented, and they often do so in response to being stroked by a human they trust, signalling their receptiveness to social contact.

However, cats may also purr when ill, injured or anxious – this explains why some cats purr frantically when being examined by a vet. Studies of the healing properties of low frequency vibrations have shown that a cat's purr vibrates at a frequency considered beneficial for bone growth, fracture healing and even pain relief. The exact significance of the purr might still be debated, but to have a purring cat on your lap is scientifically proven to be beneficial to your health, and the resonance of this low-level vibration is relaxing.

Meow is like aloha -
it can mean anything.

HANK KETCHAM

NOT A HAPPY KITTY

Anyone who has seen cats fight will undoubtedly have grasped the very real phenomenon that gave rise to the popular expression 'catfight'. Cats, usually so serene and graceful, seem to do everything in their power to avoid conflict, but when they fight, they really fight – teeth bared, fur flying and claws at the ready.

Sounds and body language often go paw-in-paw in cat communication. An arched back, fluffed up fur and sideways posture, combined with hissing and spitting, indicate a cat that is warding off a threat with offensive aggression, while a hissing cat that is crouching down indicates defensive aggression. Flattened ears and teeth exposed are other signs of an aggressive, angry or frightened cat, ready for a fight, but hoping to avoid it through sheer determined posturing. A cat with a fluffed-up tail (unless of course it belongs to a breed whose tails are naturally fluffy) is usually readying itself for a showdown and is trying to scare off an opponent.

THE SPRAY AND THE RUB

With a sense of smell 14 times stronger than your average human's, cats often use scent as a means of conveying information to other cats, both indoors and outdoors. Outdoor cats use urine spraying as a territorial marker and this is particularly true in the case of unneutered male cats, although female cats also spray on occasion. This urine tends to be thicker and more pungent than the normal, non-sprayed variety. Rubbing is another, more pleasant, form of scent-marking used by cats to make their presence known to others of their species and it's also a way of marking 'their human' and their home territory in- and outdoors with their own familiar scent.

Furniture sometimes gets 'the claw treatment' from resident cats, as cats have scent glands on their paw pads. These glands are also present on their lower back, tail, forehead, mouth, cheeks and chin, and all the friendly rubbing up against us humans is chiefly a way of marking us with their own scent.

GRACEFUL GROOMING

Cats spend up to 50 per cent of their waking hours engaging in some form of grooming. Mother cats teach their kittens to lick and wash themselves when newborn.

They lick their coats not just to keep clean and tidy, but also to waterproof their fur with the help of sebum, an oily substance secreted from the sebaceous glands at the base of each hair follicle. This helps to keep their fur shiny.

Although cats with access to water have been known to tolerate temperatures of up to 56 degrees Celsius (133 degrees Fahrenheit), cats don't sweat, except through their paws, so licking their coats can be a way for them to cool down and prevent overheating.

THE CAT'S WHISKERS

A cat's whiskers are touch receptors – something like cat radar – allowing it to feel its surroundings. The top two rows of whiskers can move independently of the bottom two. A cat has about 12 whiskers on each side of its face. If a whisker falls off, it's usually completely replaced within two to three months.

PREDATORY BEHAVIOUR

Cats, although a domesticated species, are essentially predatory in nature. Historically, they have always been great hunters, following their natural instinct to catch and kill prey in order to feed themselves and survive. They're confirmed carnivores with great stalking, pouncing and ambushing skills. Their senses, such as smell and hearing, are vastly superior to that of humans or other animals. A cat's ears can swivel independently of each other to pinpoint even the tiniest of sounds, such as the high frequency noises made by rodents.

Today, the domestic cat rarely needs to catch and kill its own prey for survival – it's long since worked out how to get its favourite treats from its human – but the predatory instincts survive. Kittens act out this instinctive behaviour in play and those growing up to become outdoor cats generally continue to chase and catch both rodents and birds, often bringing home their kill as 'presents' for their preferred humans. Cats remain natural born predators no matter how cute, cuddly and affectionate they may act towards us.

MATING

Your average frisky male cat is quite happy to mate at any time. This is, however, not so with the female, and the tomcat has to wait until he finds a female cat in season, also known as being 'in heat'. This 'heat cycle' is a short period of up to 14 days and can occur in cats as young as four to five months. The breeding seasons are usually in spring and autumn, but some cats start earlier and finish later in the year. Cats in heat have a tendency to show more affection towards their humans and will also yowl or meow loudly to attract a tom's attention. Most of the catfights of the more ferocious kind take place between males fighting over who gets to mate with a specific female in heat. Females, also known as queens, can be quite selective in terms of their choice of tomcat and may also mate with more than one during the same cycle, which means that one litter of kittens may have several different fathers.

No matter how much cats fight, there always seem to be plenty of kittens.

ABRAHAM LINCOLN

THE RIGHTING REFLEX

Who hasn't heard the expression 'a cat always lands on its feet'? The cat's righting reflex – its ability to right itself so that it lands feet first – is a well-known phenomenon. This remarkable feat is perfected before a kitten is two months old. The flexible back of a cat is made up of 53 loose-fitting vertebrae – humans have only 34. The absence of collarbones also helps a cat accomplish the twist before reaching the ground, but it still needs a minimum of 30 centimetres (12 inches) for the righting reflex to kick in properly so it can land safely. Cats relax when falling, bending the middle of their bodies while initially tucking their front legs in and extending their rear legs as they start to twist. To complete the movement, they switch their legs, extending the front and tucking in the rear. A cat in Boston, USA, called Sugar, survived a fall from the nineteenth floor with barely a scratch. Cats are a hardy bunch.

FLEHMEN RESPONSE

Cats are equipped with a second scenting mechanism, known as the vomeronasal organ, found between the palate of the mouth and the septum of the nose. This organ is connected directly to the hypothalamus of the brain. The flehmen response, which looks rather like the cat grimacing, is how the cat receives scent information, via the vomeronasal organ, about the territory it's in, such as who has been there and when. The tongue traps pheromones and transfers them to the roof of its mouth where the vomeronasal organ lets the cat 'smell with its mouth'.

HOW TO TELL IF YOUR CAT LOVES YOU

A cat will show you its affection in numerous ways – some endearing, some annoying, but nearly always adorable, even at 3.00 a.m. A discerning species, cats won't bestow their love upon just anyone. Below are a few sure signs that you're a feline-favoured human.

LOUD PURRING

True, cats can be very liberal with their purrs. They purr for all sorts of reasons, at all sorts of times, but time spent with their favourite human can bring about a certain deep-felt rumble reserved only for you; the sound of pure feline bliss.

BELLY UP

A solitary hunter such as the cat is wary of showing its vulnerable side at the best of times. A cat lying flat on its back, tummy exposed, is a true sign of trust, showing that the cat feels safe and loved in your company.

LICKING AND NIBBLING

If a cat decides to start grooming you, you're privileged. This behaviour is usually reserved for other cats and means you're well on your way to being part of the cat's innermost circle. You're becoming an honorary cat. Playful nibbling is also one of the many favours cats bestow on their preferred humans.

HEAD-BUTTING
Not a nasty football habit, being head-butted by your cat can only mean one thing – it loves you and is rubbing its scent on you to mark you as its property.

KNEADING
When your cat is trampling a specific spot, moving its paws up and down on you, also known as kneading, it is actually reliving its youth. The kneading behaviour is strong in young kittens, as it's used to aid the mother cat's milk production. When an adult cat indulges in what feels like fluffing up a pillow – but with your lap on the receiving end – it is actually expressing love and devotion.

BLINKING SLOWLY
Cats tend to only have direct eye contact with the people they know and trust, associating a direct stare with a potential threat or aggression. If your cat is looking you straight in the eye and blinking slowly, this is the ultimate sign of trust and vulnerability. The cat closing its eyes is a great sign of affection, like a cat kiss.

BRINGING GIFTS

You may not want a little dead mouse as a present, but to the cat, it is sharing its hunting successes with you. As such, it's showing you just how important you are to it.

FASCINATING FELINE FACTS

Cats can make over 100 vocal sounds; a dog can only make ten.

A cat has 17 million nerve cells in its nose.

A cat's eyes are bigger than those of most mammals, in relation to its body size. A cat can see in much dimmer light than a human and has wider peripheral vision, but doesn't distinguish colours as well.

Compared to a human, a cat has a poor sense of taste with only 473 taste buds to your 9,000. It finds it particularly hard to distinguish sweet tastes, due to a mutation in a key taste receptor.

The technical name for the hairball, sometimes formed in a cat's stomach after frequent grooming, is a bezoar.

FOR THE LOVE OF CATS

A female cat is generally right-pawed, while a male is left-pawed.

A fast-running cat can reach speeds of up to almost 50 kilometres per hour (30 miles per hour), which is faster than a human sprinter.

Primary or guard hairs are the longest cat hairs. A cat, like most mammals, also has an undercoat of secondary, medium-length hairs and finer, short hairs. The hair on a cat's belly is typically longer and the coat also varies seasonally, with the cat shedding more hairs in summer.

Kitty from Staffordshire in the UK is the oldest cat in the world to give birth. At 30, she had two kittens and over the course of her life she produced 218 offspring.

CAT BREEDS

People who don't like cats
haven't met the right one yet.

DEBORAH A. EDWARDS

Cats may all be descendants of the *Felis silvestris catus*, but over the centuries, as cats adapted to their different environments, and more recently through selective breeding – so-called cat fancy – a number of different cat breeds have developed worldwide. Cat fancy associations recognise over 40 different long- and short-haired breeds; while ordinary, non-pedigree moggies are simply divided into domestic short-haired and domestic long-haired (short-haired are far more common). Some cat fancy associations, however, divide cats into as many as 100 or more different breeds and new ones are regularly being formally recognised. Here are some of the best known and most popular.

CAT BREEDS SMALL AND LARGE

With the rise of cat fancy, cats come in an increasing range of shapes and sizes, but some breeds stand out in the diminutive, while others excel in the gigantic stakes.

The Singapura, a breed that is thought to have begun from just six cats, is considered to be the very smallest in the world, even the males don't weigh much more than 3.6 kilograms (8 pounds). This short-haired tabby is believed to have originated from Singapore, hence the name.

The Munchkin, a relatively new breed established as recently as the 1980s, has a body only slightly smaller than your average cat. However, the legs are much shorter due to a mutation in the founder cats of this breed. In effect, this is a dwarf species of cat, and there are both long- and short-haired varieties. Other so-called dwarf cat breeds include the Minskin, the Lambkin, the Bambino, the Kinkalow, the Napoleon, the Skookum and the Dwelf.

At the other side of the spectrum there is the Savannah cat, which has only been recently accepted as an official breed. A cross between a Siamese and an African Serval cat (the latter a wild species), a Savannah male weighs up to 9 kilograms (20 pounds). This exotic-looking large-eared breed is tall and slim with a spotted coat.

The fluffy and sociable Ragdoll can take up to three years to grow to its fully mature size, with males weighing up to 9 kilograms (20 pounds), and the Maine Coon can get even heavier at 11.5 kilograms (25 pounds). Both cats are long as well as heavy. Stewie, a Maine Coon from Reno in Nevada, who passed away in 2013, held the Guinness World Record for longest cat. Stewie was 123 centimetres (48.5 inches) when fully stretched out.

ABYSSINIAN

Originally thought to come from Ethiopia (formerly Abyssinia), this is one of the most popular short-haired breeds. The Abyssinian is thought to have been introduced to the UK by British soldiers in the mid or late nineteenth century.

Characterised by large, pointy ears and almond-shaped eyes, the Abyssinian has a medium-sized, graceful body. Unlike many other breeds, where the kittens are born white and gradually develop their colours, an Abyssinian cat is born with a dark coat that becomes lighter as it matures. It's playful and can be quite attention-seeking in its approach to humans, but it's also far less vocal than some of its Oriental relations.

BENGAL

The Bengal cat is a cross, or hybrid, between the Asian Leopard cat – its name stems from the Latin name for this – and the domestic cat.

Characteristically exotic-looking, this mainly short-haired breed tends to have spots, stripes and other markings reminiscent of its wilder heritage. This cat also has horizontal stripes around the eyes, adding to its striking look. Usually classed as brown-spotted or snow-spotted in terms of colouring, the markings develop during the first few months after birth. Several generations of breeding have led to a cat that has a gentler disposition than its forebears – this is a cat that loves company.

BIRMAN

Many legends surround the origins of this colour-pointed longhair. Known as the Sacred Cat of Burma, the Birman is thought to have been a Buddhist temple cat that was brought, or possibly smuggled, to France (the name stems from *Birmanie*, French for Burma), and then spread across Europe and further afield. The breed has had a fraught and rocky history. It was almost completely wiped out during World War Two, with only two Birmans left in Europe by the end of the war, and it took a few decades for the breed to recover.

Characterised by its medium-long, silky fur coat, the Birman is also distinguished by its deep-blue eyes and white gloves on its paws. A very sociable and relaxed breed, the Birman is sometimes nicknamed 'little dog' because of its habit of greeting guests and following favoured humans around.

BRITISH SHORTHAIR

The British Shorthair is a slightly posher cousin to the common domestic cat. One of the oldest cat breeds in the world, it's thought to be a mix of ancient Egyptian domestic cats, brought over by the Romans, and European wildcats.

This breed has changed and developed over the centuries. Selective breeding in the nineteenth century particularly focused on the so-called British Blue, a cat with blue-grey colouring, usually with deep orange- or copper-coloured eyes. The British Shorthair also comes in golden, bicoloured, seal-point and tortoiseshell/ calico colour combinations and the latter is almost always female. On the whole, the British Shorthair adapts well to being an indoor cat and stays even-tempered, easy-going and tolerant.

BURMESE

The short-haired Burmese, not to be confused with the Birman, hails from Thailand and Myanmar (formerly known as Burma). The modern lineage of the Burmese can be traced back to Wong Mau, the same cat imported to the USA from Burma in the 1930s, who was bred with an American Siamese.

There are currently two strands of the breed: the American Burmese and the British, or European, Burmese and both come in a variety of colours. The latter has more of a slender build and almond-shaped eyes, while the American Burmese is stockier with rounder eyes. As a breed, Burmese cats tend to be friendly and playful throughout adulthood. Their Siamese heritage means they're vocal, albeit with a somewhat softer sound than their relations. Burmese cats are considered sociable and, to a certain extent, less independent than many other breeds, needing more attention from their human friends.

As every cat owner
knows, nobody
owns a cat.

ELLEN PERRY BERKELEY

MAINE COON

The largest breed of domestic cat in existence today, the Maine Coon is one of the oldest breeds in North America and there is plenty of speculation regarding its true origins. Also known as American Longhair, the Maine Coon is particularly prevalent in the state of Maine, where it enjoys the official status of state cat. Declining in popularity during the first half of the twentieth century, it was erroneously declared extinct in the 1950s, but has since made an excellent comeback and is now the second most popular breed in the USA.

This gentle giant of a cat is generally heavy, tall and long with a soft, long- or medium-haired coat. The tail resembles that of a racoon and the warm, wavy coat means this cat is well adapted to cold weather. Not one to keep quiet, the Maine Coon is also known for impromptu, loud vocalisations.

NORWEGIAN FOREST

The Norwegian Forest cat brings feline breeds to a whole new level of fluffy. Naturally adapted to the cold climes of northern Europe, it has a double coat; the top glossy and long, the undercoat woolly and warming. Vikings are thought to have brought these strong, sturdy cats back to Norway over a thousand years ago, possibly from the British Isles, to use as mousers on their ships.

The Norwegian Forest cat has a large, bushy tail and tufty ears somewhat reminiscent of a lynx. Strong claws make this outdoors cat an excellent climber. It's a very popular breed across Scandinavia and in France.

PERSIAN

This fluffy, long-haired breed, which also includes Chinchilla and Himalayan, hails from Persia, modern-day Iran, as the name suggests, and holds the spot as most popular pedigree breed in the USA. Since arriving in western Europe in the early seventeenth century, the Persian cat has remained a favourite and received its cat fancy recognition as early as the late nineteenth century in the UK.

Persians tend to be of a quiet, docile disposition and generally cope well with a life lived indoors, even in a smaller apartment. Well known for their thick and beautiful long coats of many colours, including blue, chocolate, golden, tabby and tortoiseshell (also known as calico), Persians need regular bathing, as well as thorough and careful brushing in addition to their own natural grooming skills.

RAGDOLL

A mix of Birman/Burmese and Persian/Angora heritage, the semi-long-haired Ragdoll was developed in California in the 1960s, reaching the UK in the early 1980s, where it's currently the fifth most popular breed.

Named after its particular and peculiar habit of going limp – relaxing completely when picked up – the Ragdoll is a classic lap cat, docile, affectionate and very gentle. It's also one of the largest domestic cat breeds, particularly the male, and comes in a variety of different coat colours from lilac and chocolate to red and cream. Usually Ragdoll kittens are born white, acquiring their colour patterns at eight to ten weeks of age.

SIAMESE

This distinctive breed, native to Thailand (formerly Siam), is one of several breeds of Oriental cat. Several kittens were imported from Asia to Europe and the Americas in the late nineteenth century for breeding and it remains popular worldwide today.

The Siamese cat, known for its slender, muscular body and triangular face, has a short, glossy coat with no undercoat. Kittens are born white or cream-coloured, showing additional colours by about four weeks of age. This intelligent cat is sociable by nature and known for its piercing blue eyes and loud, persistent cries, similar to that of a human baby's. There are numerous breeds derived from the Siamese, including the Balinese, the Javanese and the Thai Bobtail.

FASCINATING
FELINE FACTS

1. The white cat permanently perched on Bond villain Ernst Stavro Blofeld's lap is a Persian.

2. The very first 'cat show' was a small sideshow at St Giles Fair in Winchester, England, in 1598, with prizes given for best mouser and best ratter. The first cat show as they are known today took place in 1871 at London's Crystal Palace, and was organised by renowned cat lover Harrison Weir, known as 'the father of cat fancy', who founded the National Cat Club in 1887.

3. The colour of a Siamese cat changes depending on body temperature.

4. Multicoloured male cats are not very common. Only one in 3,000 tortoiseshell cats is a male.

5. The colour of the coat and the crossed eyes of a Siamese cat could be determined by the same gene.

TEN MOST POPULAR CAT BREEDS IN THE USA

1. Persian

2. Maine Coon

3. Exotic Shorthair

4. Siamese

5. Abyssinian

6. Ragdoll

7. Birman

8. American Shorthair

9. Oriental

10. Sphynx

The domestic cat seems to
have greater confidence
in itself than anyone else.

LAWRENCE N. JOHNSON

TEN MOST POPULAR CAT BREEDS IN THE UK

1. Bengal cat

2. British Shorthair

3. Persian

4. Siamese

5. Ragdoll

6. Sphynx

7. Maine Coon

8. Oriental

9. Norwegian Forest

10. Burmese

FAMOUS FELINES

Dixie is smarter than my whole cabinet.

ABRAHAM LINCOLN, REFERRING TO
ONE OF HIS TWO CATS

WARTIME CATS

There are few places a cat hasn't ventured to visit and explore, from the frozen poles to outer space. Cats have been known to catch buses and boats, check in to hotels, and much more besides, all by themselves. Cats are also unsung heroes in times of war, despite carrying out their fair share of courageous deeds. This chapter takes a brief look at some cat claims to fame.

CRIMEAN TOM

In 1854, during the Crimean War, a cat known as Crimean Tom played a key role, helping the starving British and French troops survive the Russian winter during the siege of the port of Sevastopol. It was thanks to Tom that the troops were led to a substantial hidden stash of food. The storeroom, hidden behind a pile of rubble, meant there was enough food for the men to survive the winter and, with the help of Tom, several additional caches of supplies were found near the port's waterfront.

FAITH

A London-based cat called Faith, named after the church of St Augustine's and St Faith's, where she was living during World War Two, received a medal for her bravery, surviving an entire night of bombing during the Blitz and keeping her kitten safe despite the destruction of the church. Mother and kitten, which was later named Panda, were found the following day hiding in a recess of the remains of the church by Father Henry Ross with whom Faith had been living with since 1936.

ABLE SEA CAT SIMON

A wartime ship's cat, 'Able Sea Cat' Simon, serving aboard the HMS *Amethyst* won the PDSA Dickin Medal during the Yangtze Incident in 1949. The ship remained under siege for 101 days and Simon, although wounded early on, made a recovery and continued to protect the ship's food supply from mice and rodents until safely back in the UK. Poor Simon sadly died in quarantine from an infection caused by the earlier wounds and was awarded his medal posthumously. He was buried with full military honours with hundreds attending his funeral. Out of the 62 animals to be awarded the Dickin Medal, Simon is the only cat.

Who hath a better friend than a cat?

WILLIAM HARDWIN

POLITICAL ANIMALS

There's a surprising number of cats out there with political ambitions and some have even run for office and won, while others are content just to rub shoulders with, or least rub up against, glamorous politicos.

London's 10 Downing Street, home of the prime minister, is fond of cats and there have been mouse hunters in residence at Number 10 for decades. Wilberforce, the longest serving mouser (1973–1987), was succeeded by Humphrey (named after a character in the TV series *Yes Minister*) who was chief mouser in 1989–1997. A few cat-less years followed his retirement, but these days Larry has been holding the post of mouse-hunter supremo since 2011.

In Canada, Tuxedo Stan of Halifax had more ambition than catching mice and actually ran for mayor in 2012, and he's by no means the only cat to run for an official post. A cat named Morris twice ran for president of the USA, while in Sweden a fellow feline called Mickelin is the head of a political party describing itself as seriously unserious.

FAMOUS AILUROPHILES

From royalty to explorers to politicians, everyone can be found indulging in a bit of feline fancy every now and then. Politicians appear to be particularly feline-friendly and out of the elected US presidents, most of them have been proud cat owners: George W. Bush had a black shorthair called India Bush; Tom Kitten was JFK's cat; Bill Clinton adopted a stray, naming it Socks; and, further back, Abraham Lincoln had two cats called Tabby and Dixie. Philosopher Jacques Derrida had a cat called Logos that influenced his work and theories, while the prophet Muhammad's cat was called Muezza. Queen Victoria was a great lover of animals and was especially fond of her Persian, White Heather.

ANNE FRANK'S CATS

From 1942 to 1944 a young Jewish girl in Amsterdam was writing what was to become the most famous diary of all time, *The Diary of a Young Girl*. There were three cats in Anne's life: Moortje, the cat that she had to leave behind when the family went into hiding from the Nazis; Mouschi, who was in hiding with them; and, finally, Moffie, the warehouse cat, who also appears on the pages of the diary. The latter is described as a 'fat little pig', usually picking fights with Tommy, another cat (their names were also references to the German and British soldiers).

UNSINKABLE SAM

A cat originally named Oscar became known as Unsinkable Sam because of his uncanny habit to survive torpedo attacks. In May 1941, he was one of a few survivors when the German ship, the *Bismarck*, was sunk. He was rescued by British sailors, who took him on board the HMS *Cossack*, which in turn was torpedoed by the Germans in October of the same year, again with loss of life. Oscar, however, was busy using up his nine lives and also survived this torpedo attack, thereby earning his nickname. Having lost two ships, Sam was now placed on board the HMS *Ark Royal*, which incidentally had played a key role in sinking the *Bismarck*. As fate would have it, the *Ark Royal* was sunk, testing Sam's unsinkability to the limit, but he survived and still lived to meow the tale once retired on dry land.

How we behave
toward cats here below
determines our status
in heaven.

ROBERT A. HEINLEIN

FÉLICETTE, THE SPACE CAT

There are few environments that cats haven't reached by now. The first cat in space was the French kitty Félicette, also nicknamed Astrocat, who was launched into space in 1963 and luckily survived the 15-minute experience. Rumoured to be a Paris street cat, she was acquired by the French government and selected for the first space mission, carried out on 18 October 1963, when she was blasted off earth from a rocket base in the Algerian Sahara Desert. She travelled 160 kilometres (100 miles) into space with electrodes implanted into her brain, sending messages back to earth, before her capsule was parachuted back and she was safely recovered. Sadly, Félicette was not returned to the streets of Paris after her adventure, but was put to sleep a few months later, so that the electrodes could be studied further.

FASCINATING FELINE FACTS

A famous story tells of how the prophet Muhammad cut off part of the sleeve of his prayer robe, rather than wake his sleeping cat Muezza.

Oscar, from Jersey in the Channel Islands, was the first cat to receive bionic leg implants after a combine harvester chopped off his hind legs in 2009.

A ginger cat called Bob shot to fame in 2010 in *A Street Cat Named Bob*, which depicted the life of homeless busker James Bowen and Bob, the cat, on the streets of London. The heart-warming story of how Bob, a stray cat, helped James turn his life around has sold over one million copies in the UK alone and has been translated into 30 languages. The book was such a success that it was even turned into a film.

CAT WORLD RECORDS

World's largest living cat: Hercules, a liger (lion-tiger hybrid), housed at Myrtle Beach Safari in South Carolina, USA: 3.33 metres (131 inches) long, 1.25 metres (49 inches) tall and weighing in at 418 kilograms (922 pounds).

World's tallest domestic cat: Trouble, a Savannah cat from California: 48 centimetres (19 inches).

World's lightest cat: Tinker Toy, a Blue Point Himalayan, who passed away in 1997: 680 grams (1.6 pounds).

World's most well-travelled cat: Hamlet, of Toronto, Canada: travelled 600,000 kilometres (372,822 miles) by plane after accidentally remaining on board for seven weeks. Hamlet was eventually found behind a panel in the plane's fuselage.

World's richest cat: Blackie, who inherited US$25 million (£16.5 million) from his owner Ben Rea. Rea left his furry best friend everything he owned, basically disinheriting all his human relatives.

World record for owning the highest number of cats: Jack and Donna Wright, of Ontario, Canada: 689 cats in total.

CATS IN FOLKLORE AND MYTHOLOGY

There are no ordinary cats.

COLETTE

CAT TALES

There's no denying that cats have entered into the human psyche like no other species and nowhere is this more apparent than in myths and legends. Throughout the ages cats have been worshipped and venerated or, alternatively, vilified and demonised. This chapter looks at the role of the cat in worldwide mythology and folk beliefs.

ANCIENT EGYPT

Out of all the nations and societies, modern and ancient, Egypt is best known for according the cat an almost god-like status. Cats were sacred to the Egyptians, and the goddess Bast (also known as Bastet or Pasht), often depicted as a cat, was a revered deity representing motherhood and fertility. Cats were also associated with the sun god Ra and were thought to keep the sun's rays safe at night, gathering them at sunset, hence their yellow eyes.

Killing a cat, even accidentally, was punishable by death. Cats that died a natural death were often mummified and taken to Bubastis, the centre of a cat cult, whose heyday lasted some 400 years. Bubastis became a site of pilgrimage, with thousands descending on the city every year, making sacrifices to Bast at her temple. The temple's cat population was said to be on the large side, on occasion requiring the culling of kittens, which were then mummified and sold as relics. When the temple was excavated, as many as 300,000 mummified cats were found and, infamously, a large number of them were sold as fertiliser to the UK in 1888.

The idea of calm exists
in a sitting cat.

JULES RENARD

GREEK AND ROMAN MYTHOLOGY

Although not held in such high esteem as in their southern neighbour Egypt, felines regularly crop up in both Greek and Roman mythology. The Greeks are reputed to have stolen a number of Egyptian cats, bringing them to Greece to help control the rodent population on the mainland and the islands. The words ailurophile and ailurophobe (cat lover and cat hater/fearer) both derive from the ancient Greek name for Bast, Ailuros. The Greeks saw Ailuros as a version of their lunar goddess Artemis, who in Greek mythology turns herself into a cat to escape the god of wind, Typhon.

In Roman mythology, Bast was associated with Diana, goddess of wild animals and the hunt, and was the Roman equivalent of Artemis, who also had the ability to turn herself into a cat. The Romans were very appreciative of the cats' mouse-hunting skills and to this day some 300,000 feral cats roam the ancient monuments of the city of Rome, looked after by volunteer *gattare*, or cat women.

THE *GATTARE* OF ROME

Gattara or *gattare* (plural of *gattara* in Italian) is a rather unflattering term for the wonderful, crazy cat ladies of Rome who have taken it upon themselves to feed and look after the city's vast population of homeless cats. The kitties that populate the ancient landmarks of the Roman ruins have actually been declared part of the city's 'bio-cultural heritage' and as such they are officially protected by the city council.

CELTIC CAT LORE

By the eleventh century, cats could be found all across the British Isles, right up to northern Scotland. There is plenty of evidence of cats in Celtic and, in particular, Scottish mythology. This may be because of the relative abundance of Scottish wildcats, or hybrids between wildcats and domestic cats, giving rise to legends and fairy tales. The Cat Sith (or *Cait Sidhe* in Irish Gaelic) is one such fairy creature; haunting the Scottish Highlands stealing souls, this spectre was said to resemble a large black cat. There also appears to be some overlap between Cat Sith and Grimalkin, one of the witch's familiars in *Macbeth*. There are frequent stories of shape-shifting cats stalking Scotland and Ireland; these cats were often believed to be witches, having taken on the form of their familiars. Further south, in Wales, Hywel Dda, or Hywel the Good, a tenth-century medieval king, passed legislation making it illegal to kill or harm a cat. Needless to say, this was a very unusual measure at a time when cats were associated with evil, or at the very least with otherworldly powers, in Celtic mythology.

DICK WHITTINGTON
AND HIS CAT

Richard Whittington, a man who according to popular folklore owed a lot to his cat, lived in the UK in the mid fourteenth to early fifteenth centuries and was the Lord Mayor of London on three separate occasions. Although there is little actual evidence of Mr Whittington ever having owned a cat, stories abound on how his fortunes improved thanks to his feline's formidable ratting skills. Given that the first written stories about Whittington date from several hundred years after his death, it's likely that they are less than accurate. What is undoubtedly true is that these stories became well known to the point of being incorporated into popular myth and legend. The story of Dick and his cat exists in ballad form, as a prose tale, a puppet play, an opera, a pantomime and is also depicted in paintings.

NORSE SAGAS

Cats are rarely found in Norse mythology, but there are a couple of notable exceptions in the Norse sagas. Interestingly, unlike mythological cats elsewhere, none of the Nordic ones are given names. The goddess Freya (Freyja and various alternative spellings), goddess of love, fertility, hunting and warfare, is often depicted as riding a chariot driven by two enormous white felines, occasionally described as blue or grey. Despite their key role, these cats remain nameless, but in the *Edda*, a collection of old Norse poetry, they're known as Gib-cats, a word that often refers to older male cats. The magical chain, Gleipnir, used to restrain the wolf-god Fenrir, has something of a cat in it, quite literally – one of the six mysterious ingredients that make up the chain is 'the sound of a cat walking'. That must surely be the quietest ingredient of the lot. In another story, the Norse god Thor has a cat encounter of his own, when the king of the Frost Giants decides to test Thor's strength by tricking him into lifting the heavyweight serpent Jörmungandr, disguised as a gigantic cat.

MEDIEVAL MALICE

The Middle Ages were a dark period in European history, with atrocities committed all over the continent against women and cats alike. Cats, in particular black cats, were often associated with witchcraft, devil-worship and black magic, leading to them being killed *en masse* over a period of several hundred years.

Some of the superstitions about black cats linger to this day – animal rescue centres report that it's harder to rehome black cats than cats of any other colour. Initially, only black cats were seen as evil and in league with witches as their familiars, but as religious fervour reached fever pitch in the twelfth and thirteenth centuries, all cats came to be seen as evil instruments of the devil. The mass extermination of cats ironically led to the large increase in the rodent population that caused the plague, or Black Death, which spread like wildfire across Europe in the mid fourteenth century. It was the terrible spectre of the plague that helped restore Europe's ailing cat population, as people became too preoccupied with the ravages of the disease to find the time to hunt down and kill cats.

CHINESE TALES

Legends and beliefs surrounding cats differ widely across the Asian continent. In China, cats were traditionally seen as a yin animal, often associated with evil. Chairman Mao, however, is said to have approved of cats, as long as they were good mousers. Despite his own feline-sounding name, there is little evidence of Mao Zedong being an ailurophile, even though cats have been in China for a very long time. Evidence from a grave dating back over 5,000 years suggests that cats may already have been domesticated in this part of the world over 1,000 years before ancient Egypt, and cats can be found in several Chinese legends.

The most famous cat in Chinese mythology is the goddess Li Shou and her fellow cats, which, according to legend, were put in charge of the earth by the gods. Sadly, the cat goddess was busy either napping or frolicking as cats do, and she eventually had to relinquish the responsibility of looking after the planet to humans. Li Shou was worshipped as a goddess of fertility and was thought to ward off evil spirits.

JAPANESE FORTUNE CATS

It's hard to miss the ubiquitous beckoning or waving cat in the windows of Japanese shops. This cat, Maneki Neko (*neko* meaning cat), is known as a cat of good fortune or luck. Legend has it that a Japanese landlord saw a cat with its paw waving to him and, intrigued, he approached the cat to investigate further. As he did so, he narrowly missed being struck by a bolt of lightning that hit the very spot where he'd been standing only a few seconds before. The cat came to symbolise good luck and the beckoning cat is now used in Oriental shops worldwide to attract customers and good fortune in business.

Maneki Neko is one of several well-known Japanese cat legends. In another, the Bakeneko is often depicted as a supernatural, shape-shifting cat and there are many folk tales and superstitions associated with it: Bakeneko cats are said to be able to become humans and speak human words or possess and bewitch people. If the Maneki Neko brings good luck, the Bakeneko could be said to do the opposite.

TEMPLE CATS OF THAILAND AND MYANMAR

Siamese cats, hailing from modern-day Thailand (formerly Siam), were the preferred cats of the royal family and the guardians of the kingdom's Buddhist temples, perhaps accounting for a certain haughty air maintained by the breed to this day. A famous legend, of which there are several versions, tells the story of how the cats got the kink in their tails. When bathing, a royal princess would thread her rings onto the tail of her Siamese cat. The cat would then curl his tail to prevent the rings from falling off, hence the kink.

In neighbouring Myanmar (also known as Burma), legends have it that the cat Sinh saved a temple from invading Siamese troops and that the holy monks are reincarnated as Birman cats.

AN INDIAN EPIC

Indian literary epic *The Mahabharata* tells the story of Lomasa the cat and Patila the mouse, who form an unusual bond. In this story of friendship, trust and survival, Lomasa is trapped by a hunter and saved by Patila, who strikes a bargain with the cat. Lomasa protects Patila from an owl and a mongoose, while Patila in return gnaws through the leather straps that are holding the cat prisoner. It's an interesting analysis of a relationship where one party is considerably stronger than the other and could be considered a moral tale of friendship.

CAT LEGENDS OF AFRICA

Unsurprisingly, many African cat legends feature big cats rather than domestic moggies. The myth of the werecat exists in different parts of the world, but particular to the African continent are the tales of lions and leopards who can turn into humans. These are thought to be gods and goddesses in human disguise and their human offspring become shape-shifters.

The Ashanti people of Ghana treated domestic cats as full members of their tribe, allowing them to eat with their human companions and sleep inside their tents. A bit further south, in Nigeria, the cat isn't painted in quite such a good light. One Bura folk tale from the northeast of the country tells a tale from the perspective of two mice, Yizum and Nkinki, who narrowly escape being devoured by a large cat, an experience that leads Yizum, the bush mouse, to return to its original home. Across southern Africa, white lions are, according to legend, children of the Sun God, sent down to earth as gifts to humans.

After dark, all cats are leopards.

NATIVE AMERICAN PROVERB

FASCINATING
FELINE FACTS

Although this story doesn't appear in the Old Testament of the Bible, a later legend says that Noah turned to God for help to protect the food stores on board the ark and his prayers were answered. God made a lion sneeze and out popped a cat, ready to take on the boat's rat population.

In *Malleus Maleficarum*, a Catholic text from 1486 used as a tool in the witch hunts of the time, its German clergyman author, Heinrich Kramer, asserted that witches performing a demonic illusionist trick could appear to turn themselves into cats.

In the UK, cats born at the end of the blackberry season were thought to be particularly mischievous.

THE MANY LIVES OF A CAT

According to popular myth, cats are blessed with multiple lives, particularly nine, but in southern Europe this is reduced to seven, while in the Arab world, it's six. Exactly how this myth sprang up is unclear, but it's tied to cats' uncanny ability to survive everything from high falls to other potentially life-threatening circumstances. They have extremely good balance, are very flexible and often seem to sense a danger or threat before humans. As the English proverb states: 'A cat has nine lives. For three he plays, for three he strays, and for the last three he stays.'

WORLDWIDE SUPERSTITIONS ASSOCIATED WITH CATS

Around the world, cats have come to be associated with both good or bad luck and supernatural powers. There are literally hundreds of folk tales ascribing every possible attribute to the humble moggy as well as the different breeds from Siamese cats to Persians. Cats crop up as demons, familiars, goddesses, shape-shifters and even 'weathermen', with the power to predict the weather on occasion. Many of these folk tales live on in popular culture or as urban myths.

CAT SUPERSTITIONS AROUND THE WORLD

Czech Republic – burying a dead cat in a field will give you a good harvest

England – in the sixteenth century, visitors would always kiss the cat to bring good luck

France – finding a white hair on a black cat is lucky

Italy – if you hear a cat sneeze, it's a good omen

Malaysia/Indonesia – washing your cat will lead to rain

Normandy, France – seeing a tortoiseshell cat is an omen of accidental death

Russia – blue cats are considered lucky

Scotland – if you find an unknown black cat on your porch, it's a sign of prosperity coming your way

USA – seeing a white cat at night is bad luck. Dreaming of a white cat brings good luck

Wales – if a cat's eyes widen or its pupils broaden, there will be rain

TEN GENERAL CAT SUPERSTITIONS

1. Cats can predict earthquakes.

2. If a black cat sneezes on the wedding day, it means the bride will have a happy marriage (it doesn't mention the groom, however).

3. A cat sleeping on all four paws means bad or cold weather is on its way.

4. If your cat sneezes three times you will catch a cold (probably from the cat).

5. Sailors believed that throwing a cat overboard would bring all sorts of bad luck, including stormy weather.

6. In the Dark Ages, live cats were sometimes mortared into building foundations to ensure good luck, although this was hardly good luck for the cats in question.

7. Dreaming about a tortoiseshell cat means luck in business and money matters.

8. Black cats are witches in disguise.

9. If a kitten is born in May it will become a witch's cat.

10. Kicking a cat will give you rheumatism in that leg.

WEATHER SUPERSTITIONS ASSOCIATED WITH CATS

In bygone days, seafarers would base their weather predictions on the ship's cat's behaviour. A cat meowing would mean a difficult voyage, but throwing the meowing cat overboard would make things go from bad to worse, and a storm would surely follow such an action. To avoid the cat cooking up a storm by magic, it was important to keep it happy and content during the voyage. If a cat licked its fur against the grain, a hailstorm was brewing and a sneezing cat meant rain was on its way.

Not only ships' cats but also cats in general were thought to be able to influence the weather. If a cat washed their ears, people assumed that rain was on its way, particularly in Britain where, more often than not, the prediction would be correct due to sheer statistical probability.

Cats snoring meant foul weather was approaching – it could even mean seriously snowy conditions.

Sitting with their backs to the fire, cats are helpfully telling you warmer weather is on its way. Meteorologists will soon be out of work at this rate.

KASPAR, THE SAVOY CAT

Kaspar, the cat mascot of the Savoy Hotel in London, isn't actually a cat, but a wooden sculpture of a black feline. After an unfortunate incident in 1898 involving 13 people having dinner in the hotel, where the first guest to leave the table was shot and killed a few weeks later, the hotel managers decided 13 was clearly too unlucky a number and they would not allow a group of 13 to dine there again. To avoid this, they initially provided a member of staff to sit at the table if 13 guests made a booking, but this proved very unpopular. Instead they commissioned sculptor Basil Ionides to produce a 60-centimetre-tall (2-foot-tall) lucky black cat, which now sits on a fourteenth chair placed at the table for a booking of 13 people. Kaspar has also inspired the 2007 work of fiction *Kaspar: Prince of Cats* by Michael Morpurgo.

CATS IN POPULAR CULTURE

The smallest feline
is a masterpiece.

LEONARDO DA VINCI

CREATIVE CATS

Cats have a habit of inspiring creative deeds. Over the centuries, favourite felines have cropped up in countless books, songs, plays, movies and paintings. This chapter looks at some of the best known and loved.

CATS IN CHILDREN'S BOOKS AND POETRY

Of all the creative arts, literature is perhaps the most littered with kitties – the felines of fiction remain abundant almost regardless of the era, and this is particularly true for children's books. Who hasn't enjoyed the marvellously irreverent poem 'The Owl and the Pussycat', by Edward Lear, published in 1871? Another popular work written for children that's stood the test of time is *Gobbolino, the Witch's Cat*, the tale of a black kitten born to be a witch's cat, first published in 1942.

Many of our best-loved children's cat stories have come to be enjoyed by all ages – the Cheshire Cat from *Alice's Adventures in Wonderland*, Beatrix Potter's *The Tale of Tom Kitten* and *Puss in Boots* spring to mind. More recently, J. K. Rowling's extraordinarily popular *Harry Potter* series features no fewer than three recurring cats.

THE CAT IN THE HAT

The Cat in the Hat, a children's book from 1957 written by Dr Seuss, the pen name of Theodor Seuss Geisel, has turned into a children's classic. It tells the story of the Cat, dressed in a white-and-red striped hat, who visits the home of two young children, Sally and her brother (who, as the story's narrator, is nameless throughout), while their mother is away. The Cat proceeds to teach them tricks that result in wrecking their house, before putting everything right at the last minute. In the first three years after publication, *The Cat in the Hat* sold nearly a million copies and today over ten million copies in 12 languages have been sold. It's also been adapted for television, theatre and film, the latter in 2003, starring Mike Myers as the Cat.

THE CAT THAT WALKED BY HIMSELF

One of Rudyard Kipling's best-known children's stories and actually his longest story, from his *Just So Stories* collection, *The Cat that Walked by Himself* aims to explain the history of domestication. In Kipling's story the Cat, which remains nameless throughout, is the only one of the wild animals to escape domestication and retain his independence from humans. The Cat strikes a bargain with humans, but essentially he is still the cat that walks by himself when it pleases him. The poem 'Pussy Can Sit by the Fire...' ends the story.

WRITERS, ARTISTS, SINGERS AND THEIR FELINE COMPANIONS

Literary greats are often well-known ailurophiles, or cat lovers, and many in the creative professions choose a cat as their muse. Behind many a great writer there appears to be a fluffy feline or a mysterious moggy. T. S. Eliot's cat Jellylorum was featured in his *Old Possum's Book of Practical Cats*, the basis for the much-lauded musical *Cats*. Ernest Hemingway famously had a somewhat odd penchant for polydactyl, six-toed, cats and he kept a large number of them, of which Snowball is the best known, in his house in Key West. French novelist Colette and her British contemporary Virginia Woolf were both devoted to their cats. A more modern-day cat lover is American singer Taylor Swift, who often travels with her pedigree Scottish Folds.

Cats have also appeared in art for thousands of years and many artists had a special relationship with their cat companions: Salvador Dalí, Pablo Picasso, Henri Matisse and Gustav Klimt to name just a few.

THE CHESHIRE CAT

The grinning, stripy tabby of Lewis Carroll's *Alice's Adventures in Wonderland*, known for his iconic wide smile, dates back further than the story itself, which was first published in 1865. The county of Cheshire was once known for its many dairy farms and the Cheshire Cat may be related to the expression 'the cat that got the cream'. There are carvings of grinning cats in churches of the area, dating back to the sixteenth century, and already in the eighteenth century there is a mention of a Cheshire Cat in a dictionary written by Francis Grose.

The story has been adapted to the big screen, as both animated and live-action adventures, and there's even a video game featuring the world's favourite toothy feline.

CATS IN ADOLESCENT AND ADULT LITERATURE

Cats take centre stage in a number of adult works of fiction, and non-fiction, too. Nobel Prize winner Doris Lessing was an avid cat fan throughout her life and wrote several books of cat stories, including *On Cats* and *Particularly Cats*. From Edgar Allan Poe's dark mid-nineteenth-century psychological study *The Black Cat* to Greebo, the foul-tempered tomcat in the late Terry Pratchett's *Discworld* series, there is ample proof that cats appeal to both male and female authors. French novelist Colette, who was well known for her love of cats, also managed to fit them into her literary works: *Gigi* and *The Cat* were published in 1944 and 1933 respectively. Lovers of Siamese cats shouldn't miss the books by British author Doreen Tovey, who was also president of the Siamese Cat Club. She penned over a dozen books including *Cats in the Belfry* and *A Comfort of Cats*.

CATS IN ART

Painters love their moggies almost as much as writers and cat art goes all the way back to ancient Egypt, where they frequently appeared as sculptures, figurines and in engravings.

Da Vinci, who was a great animal lover, drew *Study of Cat Movements and Positions* in the early sixteenth century and, even earlier, when he was a young man in Florence, he created *Virgin and Child with Cat*. Pablo Picasso and Salvador Dalí are two of the most famous modern artists using cats in their work. The former often chose to depict their harsher, more predatory side in his paintings, such as in *Cat Eating a Bird* from 1939. Salvador Dalí took his love of cats to the wilder side and kept a pet ocelot. Dalí also collaborated with photographer Philippe Halsman in the late 1940s to create the photograph *Dalí Atomicus*, exploring the idea of suspension and featuring Dalí, along with three cats, seemingly suspended in mid-air.

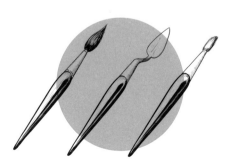

CATS IN THEATRE

No stage cats are better known than those of the eponymous musical. Composed by Andrew Lloyd Webber and based on a book by T. S. Eliot (see p.128), *Cats*, the musical, opened in the West End over 30 years ago and is still going strong. Since 1981 it's been seen by 50 million people, becoming the fourth longest-running musical in the West End and the third longest on Broadway. Telling the story of a band of cats known as the Jellicles, it's been translated into ten languages and shown on stages in over 26 countries: a true cat success story. The Tennessee Williams play *Cat on a Hot Tin Roof* deserves a pawnote, even though there are no actual cats in the play. Instead, the 'cat' in the title refers to the play's main female character, Margaret (Maggie).

There are two means of refuge from the miseries of life: music and cats.

ALBERT SCHWEITZER

CATS IN SONG LYRICS

Cats have casually sauntered into more songs than you'd think felinely possible. There has been 'Cats in the Cradle', 'The Lovecats', 'Cool for Cats' and 'Black Cat', sung by artists as different as Ugly Kid Joe, The Cure, Squeeze and Janet Jackson. Welsh crooner Tom Jones belting out 'What's New Pussycat?' has unfailingly led to the throwing of undergarments at every concert. 'What's New Pussycat?' is the title track to the film with the same name, and it's not the only film that has managed to swing a kitty into the lead song. David Bowie had a hit with 'Cat People' from the 1982 erotic horror film starring Nastassja Kinski.

More child-friendly and light-hearted is the swinging tune of 'Everybody Wants to Be a Cat' from Disney's *The Aristocats*. Interestingly, perhaps the most famous cat song of all times, 'Memory', doesn't even contain the word cat, but is sung by fictitious cat Grizabella in the musical *Cats*. 'Memory' has been recorded by over 150 artists, including superstars such as Barbra Streisand, Shirley Bassey and Elaine Page.

CATS IN FILM

Many much-read cat tales have also made it to the screen over the years, replete with our favourite furry felines as heroes and villains full of derring-do, and not just in animated films. The *Harry Potter* movies featured several real cats – incidentally Crookshanks, Hermione's cat, and Mrs Norris, caretaker Filch's cat, were both played by more than one cat star, the latter Maine Coons, the former red Persians. The white fluffy cat of Bond villain Ernst Stavro Blofeld appears in seven of the 007 movies.

Other movies with a cat theme, but where humans portray the cats, include *Cat People* and *Batman*, where Catwoman is key to the plot. Catwoman also had her very own movie, starring Halle Berry as the female feline super villainess.

Cats also make frequent appearances in animated films. Walt Disney alone is responsible for releasing *Alice in Wonderland*, featuring the Cheshire Cat, *The Aristocats* and many others. More recently, fairy tale *Puss in Boots*, also a much-lauded pantomime, has made a reappearance in the animated adventure voiced by Antonio Banderas and Salma Hayek, among others.

TV SERIES FEATURING CATS

As the interest in cats from the general public continues to rise, there's been an upswing in material relating to cats on TV, including BBC's extremely popular series *Big Cat Diary*, filmed in Kenya. While big cats have already received plenty of attention with everything from safari documentaries to feature films, the domestic cat has been lagging behind in terms of scientific study and interest. But experts have begun to pay closer attention to the lives and loves of moggies. English actress Joanna Lumley starred in the TV documentary *Catwoman* in 2009, looking at the history of the cat in different cultures, while focusing on the relationship between cats and humans over the centuries. More recently, BBC created a documentary series, *The Secret Life of the Cat*, in 2012–2013, where 50 cats in the county of Surrey in southern England were equipped with GPS collars to see what they got up to when we humans weren't watching. The trend looks set to continue – people's curiosity about their feline friends has rarely been greater.

CATS IN CARTOONS, COMICS AND ANIMATION

The field of comics and cartoons has successfully immortalised the cat over the decades. Felix the cat was one of the earliest cartoon cats in the 1920s, and, later in the 1940s, there was Tom in *Tom and Jerry*, and Sylvester the cat from the *Looney Tunes* series. Sylvester, known as Tuxedo Cat, successfully crossed over to the world of animated film and TV, for example, starring with the Big Bad Wolf in *Red Riding Hoodwinked* in 1955. In the 1960s the Hanna-Barbera Studios brought Top Cat to TV audiences in a 30-episode cat-adventure.

One of the most famous comic strips of all time is Jim Davis' *Garfield*; created in the late 1970s, it rapidly gained countless fans and holds the Guinness World Record for most widely syndicated comic. Garfield, the ultimate lazy cat who hates Mondays, struck a definite chord with the public. His fellow comic kitties include his uninterested 'love interest' Arlene and kitten Nermal. Also in the 1970s, pink-stripy cloth-cat Bagpuss debuted on television and the 13 episodes have become oft-repeated classics.

FASCINATING FELINE FACTS

Recently, Russian artist Svetlana Petrova's large ginger cat, Zarathustra, has risen to fame online, appearing superimposed on a series of well-known portraits, which includes him getting squeezed by da Vinci's Mona Lisa and draping himself across Venus of Urbino.

SOFA aka the Society of Feline Artists was created in 1994 in Leicester, UK, to promote established and up-and-coming artists specialising in the painting of cats. SOFA organises an annual exhibition in London, often featuring over 100 artists, and also hosts regional exhibitions in other parts of the UK.

The cat Marlon Brando is seen stroking in *The Godfather* was a stray that had happened to wander onto the set, accidentally making cinematic history.

Despite her looks and her very name, icon *Hello Kitty* is in fact not a cat but a girl, according to Sanrio, the Japanese toymaker behind this successful brand.

FIVE FICTIONAL EVIL CATS

1. Villain Ernst Stavro Blofeld's big fluffy white cat, in the *James Bond* films, looks deceptively cuddly until she hisses.

2. Mrs Norris, caretaker Filch's orange-eyed cat of the *Harry Potter* books and films, is always on the prowl to catch naughty Hogwarts students out of bed after hours.

3. Greebo, from Terry Pratchett's *Discworld* series, is the cat belonging to one of the Wyrd sisters. Not exactly your average cuddly kitten, Greebo manages to kill off several vampires and slay a she-wolf. He is one mean kitty-cat.

4. *Cat People*, a tale of incestuous werecats, has a veritable cornucopia of evil cats. In fact, everyone in the whole film is evil.

5. Macavity appears in both the book the musical *Cats* is based on and the musical itself, where he is the only real villain cat. He also reputedly has hypnotic powers.

THE CONTEMPORARY CAT

One must love a cat
on its own terms.

PAUL GRAY

MODERN CAT IDEAS

Along with the rise of the cat as the preferred pet, a variety of new cat-related phenomena has begun to flourish. There is such a thing as cat therapy, and for those who can't have their own cat, there are now numerous cat cafes where you can get some quality kitty time. For a final cat fix, there is a wide range of celebrity cats to enjoy on the internet. Read on to find out more about some of these modern-day cats.

CAT-SITTING

Cat owners are increasingly discovering the joys of having their cats looked after in their own homes when travelling the world, whether for business or pleasure, and pet-sitting – something akin to a live-in 'pet nanny' – has well and truly taken off. There are of course still catteries that house cats while their owners are away, but cats are notoriously resistant to change and feel happiest when allowed to stay in a familiar place.

In today's society, city- and country-dwellers alike might not know their neighbours, nor have friends living nearby, making it difficult to get someone they know and trust to come and look after their pets. Getting a cat-sitter to stay in your own home can often prove a good option. A cat-sitter, usually an avid cat lover, will stay for the duration of your absence, looking after all the cat's needs, from feeding to playing and grooming. Your cat gets to stick to its usual habits, with a minimum of disruption, while getting full-time attention from the visiting cat lover. These days, house- and pet-sitting is a booming business, with some choosing to spend all their time and make all their living from travelling the world looking after pets.

CAT THERAPY

Who hasn't heard of the horse whisperer, after the famous book and movie of the same name? But is there a cat equivalent? Yes, to some extent. The field of pet behaviour counselling is comparatively new, with the first professional body in the UK – the Association of Pet Behaviour Counsellors (APBC) – being set up in the late 1990s. It is, however, a field that's currently receiving increased recognition both from pet owners and other professionals, such as vets, who nowadays work closely with behaviourists in many cases. A cat behaviourist, as the name suggests, works with all sorts of behaviour-related problems that don't appear to be of a physiological nature, covering issues from unwanted spraying and aggression to anxiety and many others.

CAT CAFES AROUND THE WORLD

By now a worldwide craze, the so-called 'cat cafe' originated in Asia – the very first one was opened in Taipei, Taiwan, in 1998. These themed cafes, where you can not only indulge in your favourite teas or coffees but can also watch and interact with the resident cats, have spread across the globe since first opening their doors to cat lovers.

Japanese visitors to Taiwan discovered the pleasures of cat companions in cafes and were next to open cat cafes in 2004. Cats are often banned from apartments in Japan, so perhaps for that reason there are almost 40 cat cafes in Tokyo alone for cat lovers who can't keep a moggy at home. Europe, North America and Australia have since got in on the act – there are almost 20 such cafes across Europe and some 25 across North America, and the trend keeps growing. In London, Lady Dinah's Cat Emporium opened in March 2014 and Scotland has its very own Maison de Moggy since January 2015. Looks like cat cafes have come to stay.

CAT CAFE DOS AND DON'TS

Most cat cafes will have some rules to take note of while you are there. They are put in place to protect the cats' well-being and do vary slightly from cafe to cafe, so be sure to look up your individual cat cafe rules before visiting.

- Feel free to stroke, cuddle and pet the cats, or just indulge in cat watching.

- Photos are usually allowed, without flash.

- Don't restrain or pick up the cats. The pulling of tails is also not allowed, nor is it allowed to disturb sleeping cats.

- Most cat cafes outside of Asia urge you not to feed the cats, although some allow you to feed them occasional treats.

- Rule number one: if the cat wants your attention they will usually let you know. Wait and let the cat come to you.

I was only a small child when the seeds of cat enchantment were sown within me.

MAY EUSTACE

CAT CAFES WORLDWIDE

A coffee? And would you like a cat with that?

CAT CAFE HAPINEKO, TOKYO, JAPAN

The name means Cat Cafe Happy Cat and this little cafe, with 16 mostly short-haired resident cats, is tucked away on a side street in the neighbourhood of Shibuya. It's open daily until 10.00 p.m. and charges about UK£3.50 (US$5.00) for 30 minutes.

CAFE NEKO, VIENNA, AUSTRIA

Vienna's cat cafe, the first in Europe, opened its doors in May 2012. The cafe's Japanese owner serves up Japanese teas and homemade cakes.

CAT'S ATTIC, SEOUL AND BUSAN, SOUTH KOREA

Cat's Attic is a chain of popular cat cafes in nine locations throughout the South Korean cities of Seoul and Busan. Open 1.00–10.00 p.m., they can get very busy in the evenings and at weekends.

PEE PEE'S KATZENCAFÉ, BERLIN, GERMANY

Berlin's feline cafe offers plenty of entertainment for cats and humans alike, with climbing frames for the cats and free Wi-Fi for the humans.

LADY DINAH'S CAT EMPORIUM, LONDON, UK

London's first cat cafe is a cosy den, spread over two floors, with 12 resident cats, originally all rescue cats. Open daily except Wednesdays, it also runs courses and special events.

AILUROMANIA CAFE, DUBAI, UAE

The first cat cafe in the Middle East is open daily and is home to 17 cats of a variety of breeds.

LA GATOTECA, MADRID, SPAIN

La Gatoteca in Madrid is the cafe part of the non-profit organisation ABRIGA that helps to rehome cats. It's one of the few cat cafes that also have cats for adoption, as well as providing a cat-sitting service and many special events.

CAFÉ MIAO, COPENHAGEN, DENMARK

Describing itself as 'a cafe with a touch of miao' and home to nine resident cats, Café Miao serves up Chinese-inspired dishes and burgers with cat-shaped buns.

LE CAFÉ DES CHATS, MONTRÉAL, CANADA

Le Chat est Roi, or the Cat is King, is the motto at the first cat cafe to open in North America, in the French-speaking Province of Québec, in the autumn of 2014. The cafe features cats adopted from the local SPCA.

CAT TOWN CAFE, OAKLAND, CALIFORNIA, USA

Cat Town Cafe, the first cat cafe in the USA, is the cafe part of the all-volunteer cat rescue organisation Cat Town, established in 2011. They also have cats up for adoption and although booking is advised at the cafe, they also welcome drop-in guests.

CAT CAFE MELBOURNE, MELBOURNE, AUSTRALIA

Down under's first cat cafe is open daily and has 11 resident felines, as well as a shop of cat-themed gifts.

INTERNET CATS

We are truly living in the era of the internet cat, when cats with specific characteristics or looks are becoming well-known celebrities in their own right. In fact, out of everything that's happening on the internet, you sometimes get the feeling that at least 70 per cent is all about cats – but who's complaining?

Few people will have missed the now world-famous Grumpy Cat, whose real name is Tardar Sauce, known for her continuously grumpy facial expressions caused by an underbite and feline dwarfism. The internet sensation now has her own brand, has starred in her own movie and has appeared on countless TV shows.

Other internet cats include Maru, a curious and amusing Scottish Fold, who's been viewed millions of times on YouTube and runt-of-the-litter-kitty Lil Bub, with a permanently protruding tongue. These cats prove that not only cute and adorable cats make it on the internet – unusual or downright odd goes down just as well with the online cat crowd.

TOP FIVE MOST POPULAR INTERNET CATS

1. Maru, a Scottish Fold, born in Japan in 2007, never fails to *ameows* his viewers, over 200 million of them by now, to be exact. His YouTube stunts have gained him the nickname 'funniest cat on the planet'.

2. Grumpy Cat aka Tardar Sauce, born in Arizona in 2012, is known for her exceedingly grumpy face that's made her a movie and a TV celebrity.

3. Snoopy the Cat, an Exotic Shorthair and cat celebrity worldwide, particularly in China, looks more like a cuddly toy than a cat. Large orange eyes add to the look. Probably the most huggable cat in the world.

4. Nala, hailing from Los Angeles, California, is another popular Facebook cat, who's branched out. If you're a fan of this cross-eyed kitty you can get all sorts of different Nala merchandise to take home, including T-shirts and mobile phone cases.

5. Hamilton the Hipster Cat, a California rescue cat, is famous for his all-natural handlebar moustache. You can't beat this cat in a top hat.

FASCINATING FELINE FACTS

Sockington, aka Sockamillion, is a domestic cat from Massachusetts, USA, owned by tech-historian Jason Scott, who's been writing tweets from the perspective of his cat since 2007. By now Sockington has almost one and a half million followers, the most popular non-human on Twitter, and Scott has also created two other cat voices, Pennycat and Tweetie who post in relation to Sockington.

Disneyland in California, USA, is home to 200 feral cats that keep the park's vermin population in check. They prowl the park at night, and are fed, neutered and given all their shots by the park staff.

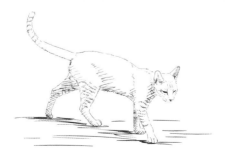

HOTEL CATS OF THE WORLD

- Poussy and his successor Carmen were known to be resident cats at Le Negresco hotel in Nice, France. The former is said to have mostly hung out in the hotel bar.

- Matilda (when female) and Hamlet (when male) have taken turns as resident hotel cats at the Algonquin Hotel in New York since the 1930s.

- Le Bristol hotel, in Paris, has had two adorable Burmese cats since 2010, Fa-raon and Kléopatre.

- Two strays named Whisky and Soda used to make the Belmond Mount Nelson Hotel in Cape Town, South Africa, their home.

- One of the best-known cat hotels of all time, the Anderson House Hotel in Minnesota, where you could either bring your own cat or spend time with the 15 in residence, sadly changed management, and thereby also cat policy in 2011, and cats are no longer allowed in the rooms.

What greater gift than
the love of a cat?

CHARLES DICKENS

RESOURCES

Brown, Milly *The Cat Lover's Compendium* (2013, Summersdale)

Budiansky, Stephen *The Character of Cats: The Origins, Intelligence, Behaviour and Stratagems of* Felis silvestris catus (2003, Penguin Books)

Dosa, David *Making Rounds with Oscar: The Extraordinary Gift of an Ordinary Cat* (2011, Hyperion)

Heath, Sarah *Why Does my Cat…?* (2000, Souvenir Press)

Mash, Holly *The Holistic Cat: A Complete Guide to Natural Health Care* (2014, The Crowood Press)

Morgan, Ashley *Wonder Cats: True Tales of Extraordinary Felines* (2010, Summersdale)

Page, Jake *Do Cats Hear with Their Feet? Where Cats Come from, What We Know about Them, and What They Think about Us* (2008, Harper Collins)

Riccomini, Francesca *Cat Care Essentials* (2010, Hamlyn)

FURTHER READING

CAT BREEDS

www.catster.com/cat-breeds/most-popular-cat-breeds

CAT CARE

www.bluecross.org.uk

www.thecatsite.com

CAT PROTECTION AND ADOPTION

www.cats.org.uk

www.catchat.org

www.rspca.org.uk

CAT-SITTING

www.trustedhousesitters.com/gb

www.housesittingworld.com

THE CONTEMPORARY CAT

www.apbc.org.uk

TRIVIA/GENERAL

www.moggies.co.uk

www.catquotes.com

www.catster.com

WILDCATS

www.bigcats.com/cat-species-weight-comparison

FOR THE LOVE OF DOGS

Kate May

ISBN: 978 1 78685 032 4

£9.99

To sit with a dog on a hillside on a glorious afternoon is to be back in Eden.

MILAN KUNDERA

Far above and beyond their loyalty and devotion, we love dogs all the more for their individual quirks and personalities – the funny sideways look they give you when you talk, the face-lick when you're sad, the way they will chase a glimmer of light and yet stubbornly refuse to fetch a ball...

PACKED WITH FASCINATING FACTS AND TRIVIA, HEART-WARMING STORIES AND INSPIRING QUOTES, *FOR THE LOVE OF DOGS* IS PERFECT FOR ANYONE WHO VALUES THE TRUSTY COMPANIONSHIP OF THEIR FAVOURITE POOCH.

Have you enjoyed this book?
If so, why not write a review on your
favourite website?

If you're interested in finding out more
about our books, find us on Facebook at
Summersdale Publishers and follow us on
Twitter at @Summersdale.

Thanks very much for buying this
Summersdale book.

www.summersdale.com